SCYC
8-09

The Migration of a Butterfly

Of a

Written by
Tanya Kant

Illustrated by
Carolyn Franklin

Hold the page
up to the light
to see what's on
the other side.

children's press®
An Imprint of Scholastic Inc.
NEW YORK • TORONTO • LONDON • AUCKLAND • SYDNEY
MEXICO CITY • NEW DELHI • HONG KONG
DANBURY, CONNECTICUT

Published in Great Britain in 2008 by
The Salariya Book Company Ltd
25 Marlborough Place, Brighton BN1 1UB
England
www.salariya.com
ISBN-13: 978-0-531-24048-9 (lib. bdg.)   978-0-531-23802-8 (pbk.)
ISBN-10: 0-531-24048-7 (lib. bdg.)   0-531-23802-4 (pbk.)
All rights reserved.
Published in 2009 in the United States
by Children's Press
An imprint of Scholastic Inc.

A CIP catalog record for this book is available
from the Library of Congress.

Author: **Tanya Kant** is a graduate of the University of Sussex at Brighton, England. She specializes in writing and editing children's nonfiction, and is especially interested in natural science and history. She lives in Hove, England.

Artist: **Carolyn Franklin** is a graduate of Brighton College of Art, England, specializing in design and illustration. She has worked in animation, advertising, and children's fiction and nonfiction. She has a special interest in natural history and has written many books on the subject, including *Life in the Wetlands* in the **WHAT ON EARTH?** series and *Egg to Owl* in the **CYCLES OF LIFE** series.

Consultant: **Monica Hughes** is an experienced educational advisor and author of more than one hundred books for young children. She has been headteacher of a primary school, primary advisory teacher, and senior lecturer in early childhood education.

monarch butterfly

**PAPER FROM
SUSTAINABLE
FORESTS**

Printed and bound
in China.

Contents

monarch butterfly

wing

thorax

eye

head

abdomen

leg

tongue

4

What Is a Butterfly?

A butterfly is an **insect** with two pairs of large, patterned wings and a pair of **antennae**. An insect has three parts to its body: a head, a **thorax**, and an **abdomen**. The thorax is the middle part of an insect's body. The abdomen is its tail part. All insects have six legs.

antennae

Butterflies have long, curly tongues that they unroll to suck up **nectar** from the middle of flowers.

What Does "Migration" Mean?

Migration is the movement of a group of animals to a different place for part of the year. In the fall, many thousands of monarch butterflies fly from Canada and the northern United States all the way to Mexico, Florida, and California. They spend the winter there, resting. In the spring, they lay their eggs. Their **offspring** fly back to the northern United States and Canada.

Monarch butterflies can also be found in Australia, in New Zealand, and on the west coasts of Europe and Africa. In Australia they are often called **wanderer** butterflies.

In this book you can follow the amazing migration of the monarch butterflies of North America.

monarch butterflies migrating

Flutter flutter

Why Do Monarch Butterflies Migrate?

Monarch butterflies migrate because they like warm weather. In the summer, many monarch butterflies live in Canada and the northern United States. They spend all summer feeding there. In the fall, the weather turns colder and there is less food for them to eat. So the butterflies fly south, where it is warmer.

fall leaves

A monarch butterfly has big, strong wings. It can fly quickly and for very long distances.

strong wings

9

How Do the Butterflies Make Their Journey?

Butterflies gather in groups to start their migration. More and more butterflies join each group. Soon there are thousands of butterflies all flying together. They can fly up to 45 miles in one day!

At night, the butterflies land on trees to rest. Each morning they continue flying south.

The butterflies rest at night.

When Do the Butterflies Reach the South?

The butterflies reach the south in the early winter. Thousands and thousands of them settle on the trunks and branches of trees. The butterflies will rest all through the winter. This is called **overwintering**.

Thousands cluster together.

Year after year, new butterflies **cluster** together on the same trees.

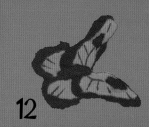

How Long Do the Butterflies Rest?

The butterflies stay in the south until spring, when the weather begins to get warmer. In February or March they set off on their return journey toward the north.

The butterflies fly back in spring.

Monarch butterflies do not fly back in big groups. Each butterfly sets off alone.

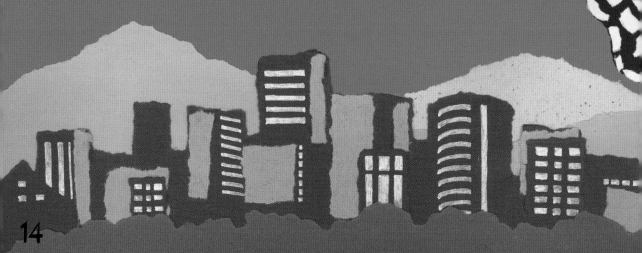

Each butterfly flies back alone.

What Happens on the Journey North?

Before and during their journey north, female and male butterflies meet up in pairs to **mate**. After a female butterfly's eggs have been **fertilized**, she stops to lay her eggs on a leaf. After their eggs have been safely laid, the adult butterflies die. Their offspring will complete the journey to the north.

milkweed plant

The female butterfly looks for a **milkweed** plant. She lays her eggs on the undersides of leaves. She makes a sticky substance that holds the egg to the leaf.

A **caterpillar** grows inside each egg. The caterpillar will one day become a butterfly.

female butterfly

sticky egg

milkweed plant

monarch butterfly egg

hard, gray eggshell

The eggs usually take between four and nine days to **hatch**. After the caterpillars hatch, they start to feed. First they eat their own egg. After that, monarch caterpillars feed only on milkweed plants.

18

What Hatches from the Egg?

A caterpillar hatches from the egg. Caterpillars are crawling insects with no wings and short legs. They don't look like butterflies at all.

monarch butterfly egg

Hold this page up to the light to see a caterpillar hatching.

Why Do the Caterpillars Eat Milkweed Plants?

Milkweed is poisonous to most animals. When caterpillars eat milkweed plants, they become poisonous too. Other animals usually avoid eating them.

egg

caterpillar hatching

Monarch caterpillars are pale gray when they first hatch. When they are fully grown, they have brightly colored stripes.

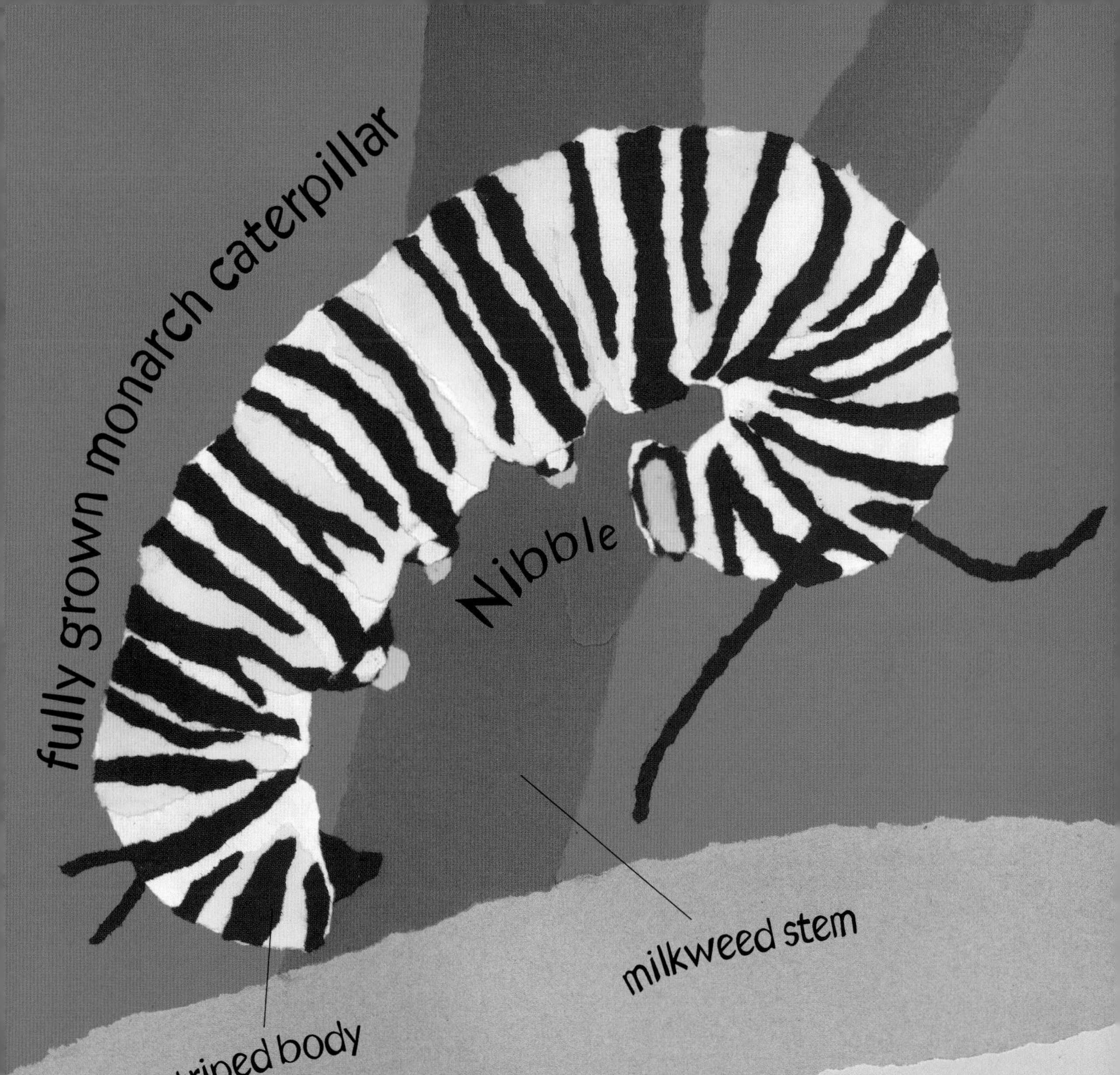

fully grown monarch caterpillar

Nibble

milkweed stem

striped body

Like the caterpillar, the
monarch butterfly is poisonous.
Its brightly colored, patterned
wings warn **predators** that it is
not a tasty treat.

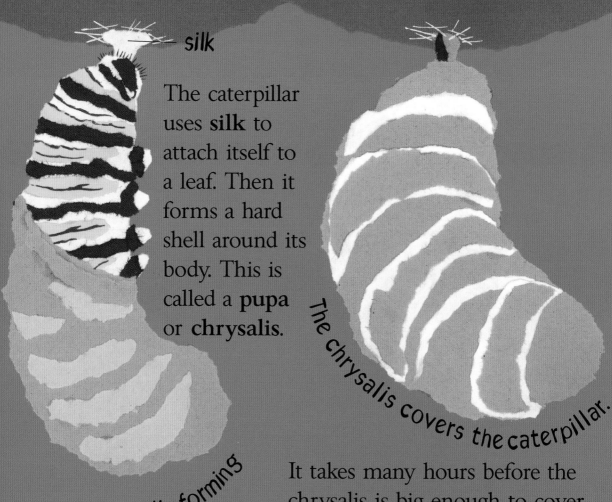

silk

The caterpillar uses **silk** to attach itself to a leaf. Then it forms a hard shell around its body. This is called a **pupa** or **chrysalis**.

chrysalis forming

The chrysalis covers the caterpillar.

It takes many hours before the chrysalis is big enough to cover the caterpillar from head to tail.

When Does a Caterpillar Turn Into a Butterfly?

As the caterpillar grows, its skin becomes very tight. From time to time it has to grow a new, bigger skin. When the caterpillar is fully grown, it is ready to turn into a butterfly.

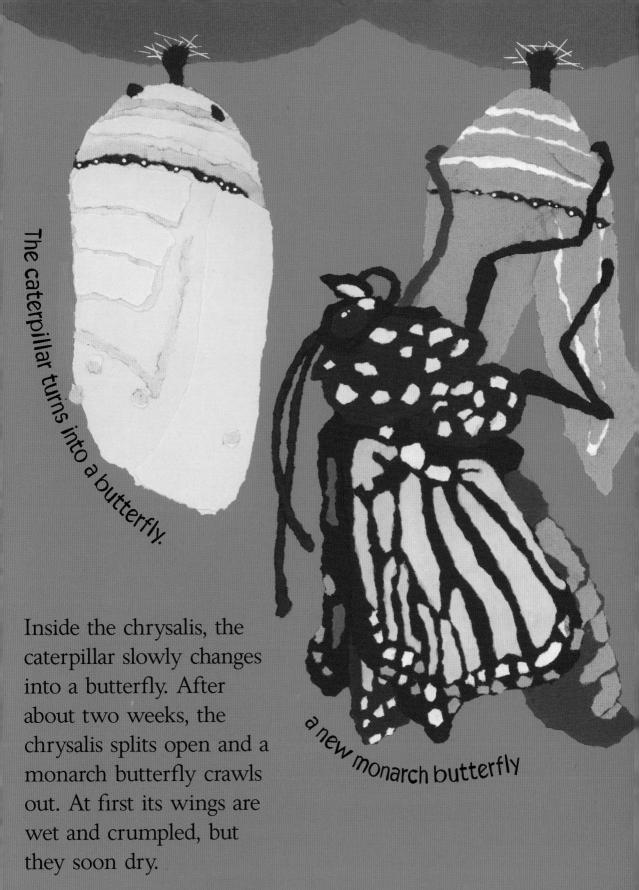

The caterpillar turns into a butterfly.

a new monarch butterfly

Inside the chrysalis, the caterpillar slowly changes into a butterfly. After about two weeks, the chrysalis splits open and a monarch butterfly crawls out. At first its wings are wet and crumpled, but they soon dry.

Where Do the Young Butterflies Go?

When the young monarch butterflies are ready, they fly back to where their parents came from—the northern United States or Canada. When they arrive, the great migration is over.

The monarch butterflies that reach Canada and the northern United States are the offspring of the butterflies that left there in the fall.

The butterflies live in the
north throughout the summer.
In the fall, it will be their turn
to fly south, and the great
migration will start once again.

The young butterflies return to the north.

Caterpillar to Butterfly

egg

adult
butterfly

newly hatched
caterpillar

pupa, or
chrysalis

fully grown caterpillar

How Long Do Monarch Butterflies Live?

If a monarch butterfly hatches in early summer, it does not migrate. It lives for only two to five weeks. Monarch butterflies that hatch in late summer do migrate. They can live for as long as nine months.

Some butterflies live for months.

Migration Map

This map shows how far the monarch butterflies travel each year on their great migration. The butterflies fly from Canada and the northern United States to California, Florida, and Mexico in the south.

Where in the world do monarch butterflies live?

Most monarch butterflies live in North America. Smaller numbers of monarch butterflies live in other parts of the world, such as Australia, New Zealand, and the west coasts of Europe and Africa.

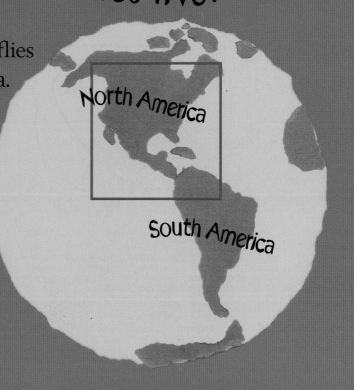

North America

South America

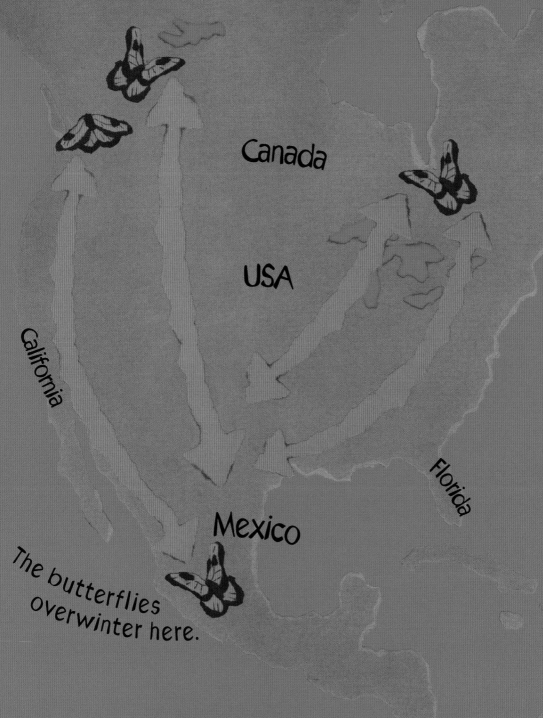

Canada

USA

California

Florida

Mexico

The butterflies overwinter here.

During their migration, the monarch butterflies fly more than 2,000 miles across North America. The journey takes them about two months.

Words to Remember

Abdomen The tail section of an insect's body.

Antennae The feelers on an insect's head.

Caterpillar A crawling insect that hatches from a butterfly's egg. When the caterpillar is fully grown it changes into a butterfly.

Chrysalis The case inside which a caterpillar turns into a butterfly.

Cluster To gather together in a close group.

Fertilized An egg is fertilized when a male and a female animal mate. Only a fertilized egg can grow into a new animal.

Hatch A caterpillar hatches when it comes out of its egg. An egg hatches when a caterpillar comes out of it.

Insect An animal that has six legs and a body made up of three sections: head, thorax, and abdomen.

Mate (noun) A partner of the opposite sex.

Mate (verb) To join together to fertilize an egg.

Migration The movement of a group of animals to a different part of the world for part of the year.

Milkweed A tall, green plant that is eaten by some insects, including monarch caterpillars. Some kinds of milkweed are poisonous. Caterpillars that eat milkweed become poisonous too.

Nectar A sweet substance in flowers that butterflies and some other insects drink.

Offspring The young produced by a pair of animals.

Overwintering Resting through the winter.

Predator An animal that kills and eats other animals.

Pupa Another word for chrysalis.

Silk A sticky substance produced by some insects. It dries to make a very thin, strong thread.

Thorax The middle section of an insect's body. An insect's legs are attached to its thorax.

Wanderer An Australian name for the monarch butterfly.

Index